Dinosaur Colors

by David West

Crabtree Publishing Company
www.crabtreebooks.com

Author: David West
Editor: Crystal Sikkens
Editorial director: Kathy Middleton
Prepress technician: Margaret Salter
Cover design: Margaret Salter
Image credits: David West; Shutterstock: p 23 (bottle)
Cover credits: Shutterstock (background); David West

Published in 2013 by CRABTREE PUBLISHING COMPANY

All rights reserved. No part of this publication may be reproduced, stored in a retrieval system or be transmitted in any form or by any means, electronic, mechanical, photocopying, recording, or otherwise, without the prior written permission of Crabtree Publishing Company. We acknowledge the financial support of the Government of Canada through the Canada Book Fund for our publishing activities.

Copyright © 2010 TickTock Entertainment Ltd.

Library and Archives Canada Cataloguing in Publication

West, David, 1956-
 Dinosaur colors / David West.

(I learn with dinosaurs)
Issued also in electronic formats.
ISBN 978-0-7787-7454-9 (bound).--ISBN 978-0-7787-7459-4 (pbk.)

 1. Colors--Juvenile literature. 2. Dinosaurs--Juvenile literature.
I. Title. II. Series: West, David, 1956- I learn with dinosaurs

QC495.5.W39 2013   j535.6   C2012-908499-9

Library of Congress Cataloging-in-Publication Data

West, David, 1956-
 Dinosaur colors / David West.
   pages cm. -- (I learn with dinosaurs)
 ISBN 978-0-7787-7454-9 (reinforced library binding : alk. paper) -- ISBN 978-0-7787-7459-4 (pbk. : alk. paper) -- ISBN 978-1-4271-9333-9 (electronic pdf) -- ISBN 978-1-4271-9321-6 (electronic html)
 1. Dinosaurs--Juvenile literature. 2. Colors--Juvenile literature. I. Title.
 QE861.5.W47 2013
 535.6--dc23

                    2012049601

Printed in Canada/012013/MA20121217

Crabtree Publishing Company

www.crabtreebooks.com   1-800-387-7650

Published in Canada
Crabtree Publishing
616 Welland Ave.
St. Catharines, Ontario
L2M 5V6

Published in the United States
Crabtree Publishing
PMB 59051
350 Fifth Avenue, 59th Floor
New York, New York 10118

Published in the United Kingdom
Crabtree Publishing
Maritime House
Basin Road North, Hove
BN41 1WR

Published in Australia
Crabtree Publishing
3 Charles Street
Coburg North
VIC, 3058

White

An Antarctosaurus and William are walking in the snow.

The snow turns everything white.

Antarctosaurus ant-ARK-tuh-SAWR-us

Black

The sky at night is black.

Dilophosaurus   dye-LO-fuh-SAWR-us

4

The Dilophosaurus and Aadi are looking for shooting stars.

Gray

Billy nearly bumps into an Ankylosaurus while riding in the fog.

Gray is made from mixing black and white.

Ankylosaurus

ang-KILE-uh-SAWR-us

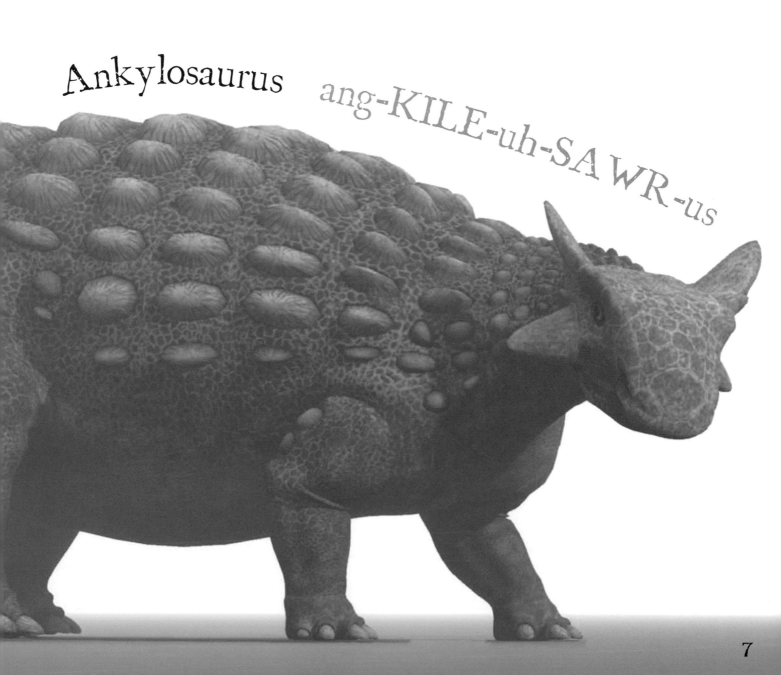

Red

Mia's uncle is painting the wall red and yellow...

But look out! The Deinonychuses have come to help out.

dye-NON-ik-us

Deinonychus

Orange

They have mixed the red and yellow paint.

Red and yellow
make orange.

Blue

The Hypsilophodon has a blue face. What is he looking at?

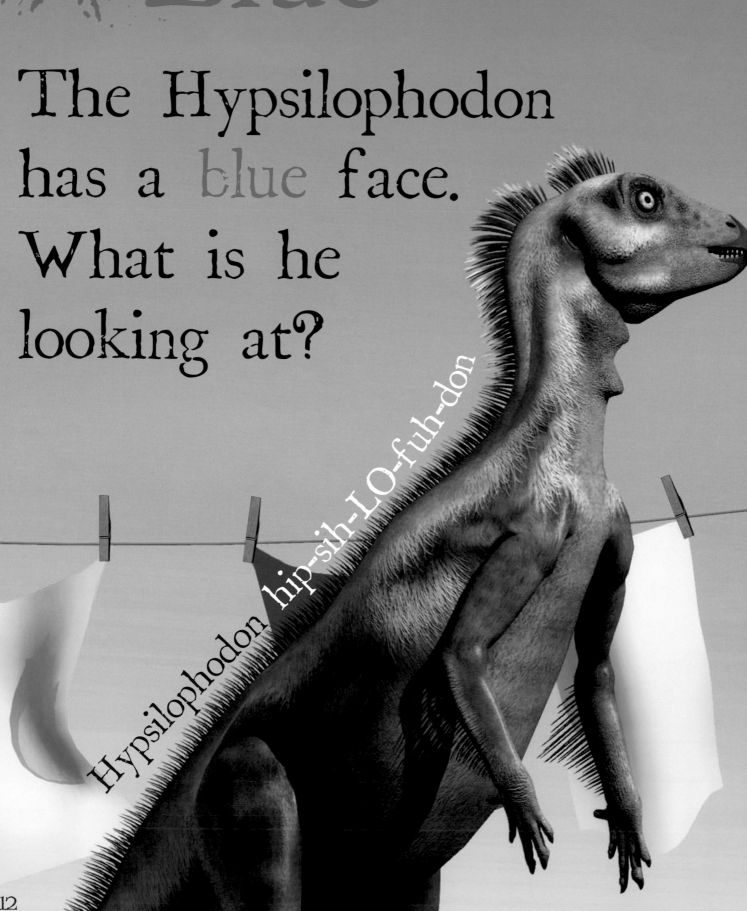

Hypsilophodon hip-sih-LO-fuh-don

It's a blue dragonfly.

Green

Alison's mom is painting an Olorotitan.

She mixes yellow and blue paint together to make green.

Olorotitan   Oh-LOW-ruh-tye-tan

15

Purple

Ethan is painting the chair the same color as the Troodon.

He mixes red and blue paint to make purple.

Troodon

TRO-uh-don

Rainbow

Brad and the three baby Camarasauruses watch Brad's dad.

Camarasaurus

kuh-MARE-uh-SAWR-us

He uses all the colors
to paint a rainbow.

Brown

The dinosaurs want to join in the fun!

They mix all the paints together and make the color brown.

Pink

The pink Juravenators want some milk, too.

Juravenator   JOO-ruh-ven-AY-tor

Mixing white milk and red strawberry syrup makes the drinks pink.

The color chart
shows you how to
mix all the colors.

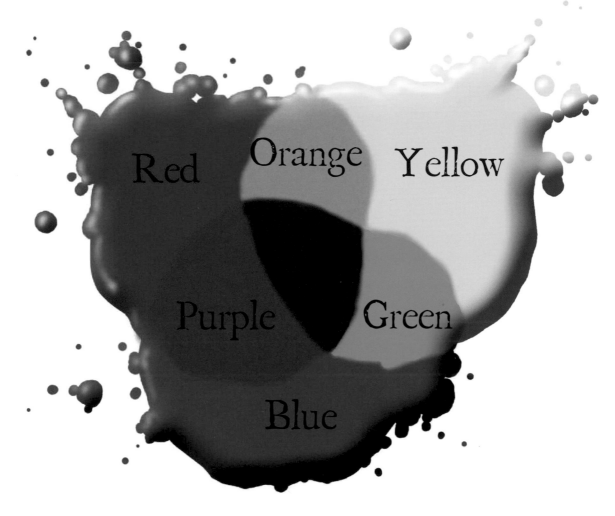

Red   Orange   Yellow

Purple   Green

Blue

Now you can make the
colors you want to paint
your own dinosaur.

+
535.6 W

West, David 1956
Dinosaur Colors /
Melcher PICTURE-BK
04/14

DISCARD